JANET BRENNER MICHAEL GILL DARYL ROTH

PRESENT

Y0-BVQ-267

Closer Than Ever

STARRING
(IN ALPHABETICAL ORDER)

BRENT BARRETT SALLY MAYES
RICHARD MUENZ LYNNE WINTERSTELLER

LYRICS BY
RICHARD MALTBY, JR.

MUSIC BY
DAVID SHIRE

CONCEIVED & CO-DIRECTED BY
STEVEN SCOTT SMITH

SCENIC DESIGN
PHILIPP JUNG

COSTUME DESIGN
JESS GOLDSTEIN

LIGHTING DESIGN
NATASHA KATZ

CASTING CONSULTANTS
JOHNSON-LIFF & ZERMAN

MUSIC PUBLISHER
TOMMY VALANDO

ASSOCIATE PRODUCER
BRYAN BURCH

MUSICAL DIRECTION & ADDITIONAL VOCAL ARRANGEMENTS BY
PATRICK SCOTT BRADY

MUSICAL STAGING BY
MARCIA MILGROM DODGE

DIRECTED BY
RICHARD MALTBY, JR.

"CLOSER THAN EVER" WAS DEVELOPED AT THE
WILLIAMSTOWN THEATRE FESTIVAL.

Original Cast Album on RCA Records and Tapes

© 1997 Alfred Publishing Co., Inc.
All Rights Reserved

DAVID SHIRE, in addition to *Closer Than Ever*, wrote the music for the Broadway musical *Baby*, which received seven Tony nominations including Best Musical and Best Score, and for the off-Broadway revue *Starting Here, Starting Now*, which has had more than 450 productions worldwide. He composed the songs and incidental music for the Joseph Papp directed New York Shakespeare Festival production of *As You Like It*, for the original Broadway production of Peter Ustinov's *The Unknown Soldier and His Wife* and the music for The Manhattan Theatre Club's *The Loman Family Picnic*. His 40 feature film scores include those for *The Conversation; All The President's Men; Norma Rae; Farewell, My Lovely; 2010; Return to Oz; Vice Versa; Short Circuit; Monkey Shines;* and *'Night Mother*. In 1980, he received two Academy Award nominations and won an Oscar for the song "It Goes Like It Goes" from *Norma Rae*. His many television scores, including those for "The Woman of Brewster Place," "Raid on Entebbe," "Do You Remember Love?", "The Kennedys of Massachusetts" and "Promise," have earned him four Emmy nominations and his recorded songs include Barbra Streisand's "What About Today?" and the international hit "With You I'm Born Again." He has also won two Grammy Awards for his contributions to the *Saturday Night Fever* album.

RICHARD MALTBY, JR. won the 1978 Tony Award as Best Director of a Musical for conceiving and directing *Ain't Misbehavin',* which also won the Tony Award and the New York Drama Critics' Circle Award as Best Musical of 1978. He directed and, with Don Black, did the American adaptation for Andrew Lloyd Webber's *Song and Dance* on Broadway, which won a Tony Award for its star, Bernadette Peters. He directed and wrote the lyrics for the 1977 Off-Broadway musical hit *Starting Here, Starting Now* with music by David Shire, the RCA original cast album of which was nominated for a Grammy Award. He collaborated with David Shire again in 1983 on the Broadway musical *Baby*, for which Mr. Maltby directed and wrote the lyrics. He directed the record-breaking Philadelphia Drama Guild productions of *Long Day's Journey into Night* and *The Glass Menagerie*, both starring Geraldine Fitzgerald, for whom he also directed a highly successful one-woman show called *Street Songs*. Mr. Maltby has a 15 year association with the Manhattan Theatre Club, where he directed *Livin' Dolls* and *Hang on to the Good Times*. The son of the well-known orchestra leader, Mr. Maltby also contributes devilish crossword puzzles to *Harper's* magazine. Mr. Maltby is co-lyricist of *Miss Saigon* which opened in London in September 1989, two months before *Closer Than Ever* opened in New York.

MUSICAL NUMBERS

NOTE: Five songs written for *Closer Than Ever* were interpolated into *Urban Blight* which was produced by the Manhattan Theatre Club. *Patterns*, though written for *Baby* and included on its cast album, was not in the show during its Broadway run.

INSTRUMENTATION FOR THE ORIGINAL STAGE PRODUCTION

Piano
Bass (acoustic and electric - 1 player)

NOTES

This score was prepared from the composer's piano copy and is identical with that used for the original New York stage production. Certain details, including many of the indicated tempi, are not the same as those on the RCA Victor original cast recording. For stage productions, this vocal score is to be considered correct.

The vocal part of MAN 3 is intended to be performed by the pianist.

The authors wish to thank Steven Scott Smith for his part in initiating and developing this project.

The composer wishes to thank Patrick Scott Brady for his assistance in the preparation of this vocal score.

In some productions, the song included in the Appendix, *I'll Get Up Tomorrow Morning*, is substituted for No. 6, *Like A Baby*, which was dropped from the New York production shortly after the show opened.

This vocal score was prepared by PAUL McKIBBINS.

The purchase of this score does not constitute permission to perform. Applications for performance of this work, whether legitimate, stock, amateur or foreign should be addressed to the licensing agent.

4

No. 1 DOORS
(COMPANY)

Lyrics by
RICHARD MALTBY, Jr.

Music by
DAVID SHIRE

WOMEN

yet there's a light   that   I'm   head - ing   for.

MEN

head - ing   for.   It's

yet there's a light   that   I'm   head - ing   for.

cresc.

Clo - ser than ev - er,   ev - er...

cresc.   Clo - ser than ev - er.

clo - ser than ev - er.   Clo - ser and clo - ser and   clo - ser and clo - ser and...

Clo - ser and clo - ser and   clo - ser and clo - ser and...

Clo - ser than ev - er.   Clo - ser and clo - ser and   clo - ser and clo - ser and...

(chime-like)

Moderato, very rhythmically (♩ = c. 96)

WOMAN 2:

Fresh out   of bed,   your life___ is out - rac - ing you.   There dead a - head, an - oth - er one's fac - ing you.

ALL:
Doors to keep out __ the chill __ of night. __ Doors to keep se - crets locked __ up tight. __

WOMEN: *(unis.) cresc.*
Just when you have __ things set, __ When it's all __ in place, __ When your life __ is good, __ There's an - oth - er

MEN: *(unis.) cresc.*
Just when you have __ things set, __ When it's all __ in place, __ When your life __ is good, __ There's an - oth - er. . .

sub. p
door. _____

mf
Door-ways are good, they can __ be en - light - en - ing, Door-ways can change you, which __ is - n't fright - en - ing.

So tell me why my stom - ach is tight - en - ing Look-ing at an - oth - er door. _____ A

WOMAN 1, MAN 1:

fff

Just when you have things set, When your life is good, When it's all in place, There's an oth - er

WOMAN 2, MAN 2:

fff

Just when you have things set, When your life is good, When it's all in place, There's an oth - er

door.

door.

fff

Ev - 'ry day an - oth - er door!

fff

Ev - 'ry day an - oth - er door!

No. 2 SHE LOVES ME NOT
(WOMAN 1, MAN 1 and MAN 2)

Lyrics by
RICHARD MALTBY, Jr.

Music by
DAVID SHIRE

Moderately bright (♩ = c. 120)

No.3 YOU WANNA BE MY FRIEND

(WOMAN 2 and MAN 2)

Lyrics by
RICHARD MALTBY, Jr.

Music by
DAVID SHIRE

Some - one who's in tune.___ And since I'll be thir - ty - nine___ next month, I

want him rath - er soon.___ I want some - one to buy rugs and lamps with,

Some - one who'll co - sign. I want a small joint bank ac - count___ in

his name and in mine.___ I need some - one I can fight___ with, Learn to

cook with, Love to feed. Come to think of it, There's on - ly one thing

28

No. 4 WHAT AM I DOIN'?

(MAN 1)

Lyrics by
RICHARD MALTBY, Jr.

Music by
DAVID SHIRE

36

No. 5 THE BEAR, THE TIGER, THE HAMSTER AND THE MOLE

(WOMAN 1)

Lyrics by
RICHARD MALTBY, Jr.

Music by
DAVID SHIRE

32 earth. And from moose to eel, What my stud-ies most re-veal Is the

35 male's in-flat-ed worth. (mf) For in most of the an-i-mal king-

p molto legato   cresc. poco a poco

38 dom,— The la-dies on-ly sel-dom need men. Their

41 cresc. deal-ings are straight.— They meet them to mate— And nev-er see— them a-

mf cresc.

44 f gain.— The bear,— the ti - ger, the ham-ster and the mole—

48

Have fe - males who live fruit-ful lives ___ out - side of male con-trol. ___

52

For one mind - less spa - sm ___ They al-

55

mf

low the male his role. ___ That's mar - riage for the

58

mf

ti - ger, bear and ham - ster. ___ Now the

ff

61

mole, who's blind, Will nev - er be con-fined to one male she's mere - ly

mf

146

(She realizes she has revealed more of

Of _____ me. _____

149 *herself than she intended; she composes herself)*

Now, of course, if fate should

152

put up-on my plate That quint - es - sen - tial male, I would

155

stick like glue, Yes, I would be as true as an-y beav-er, owl or

158

whale. But till then I'll en-vy the oys-ter, _____ Who

No. 6 LIKE A BABY

(MAN 2, WOMAN 1 and WOMAN 2)

Lyrics by
RICHARD MALTBY, Jr.

Music by
DAVID SHIRE

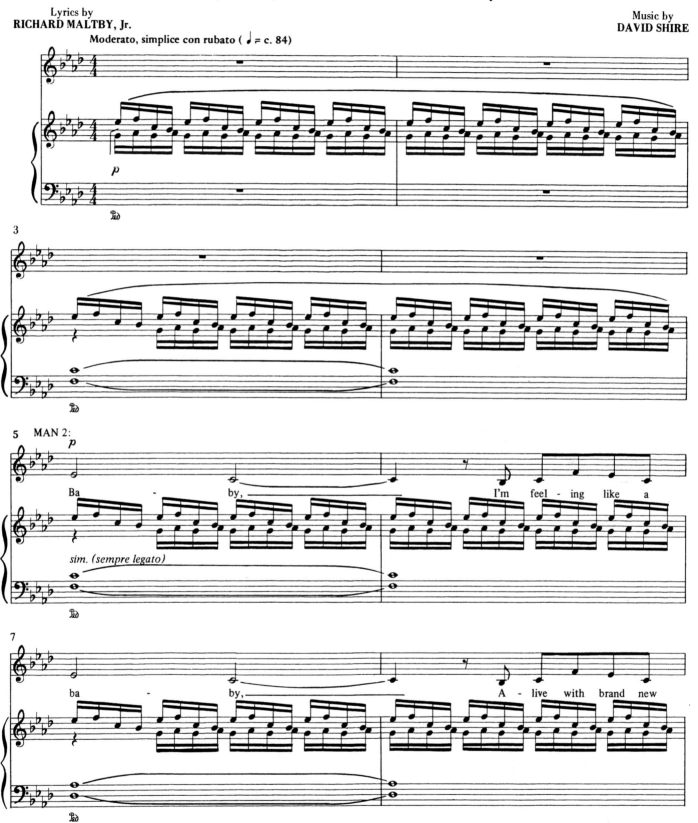

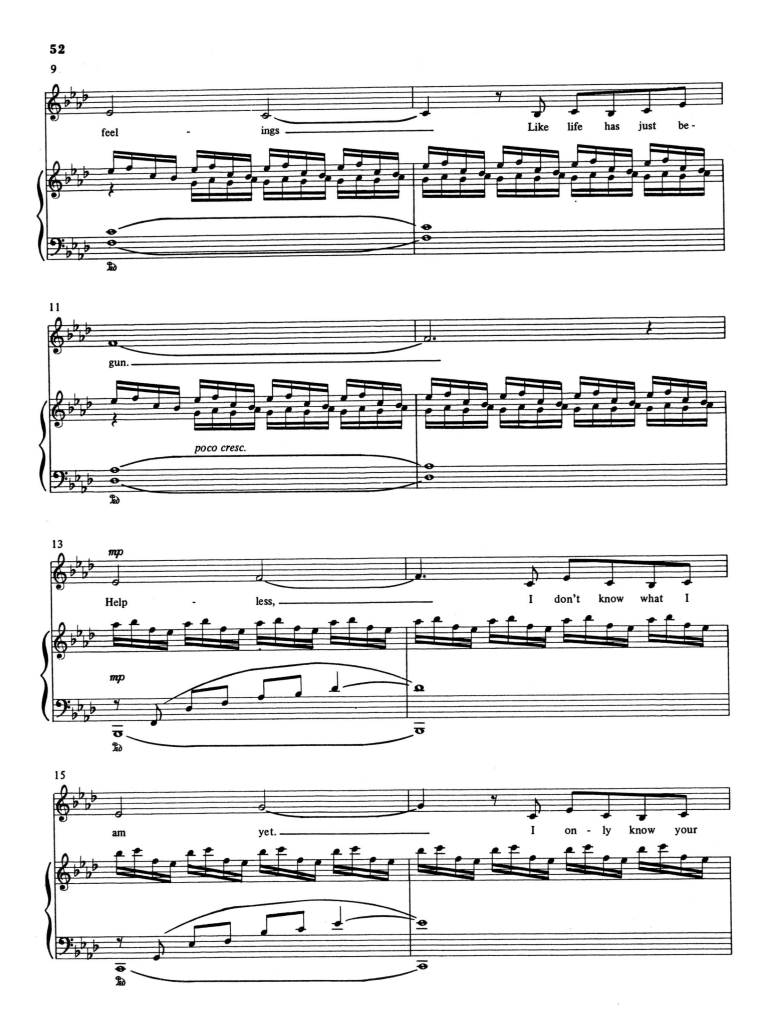

54

58

No. 7 MISS BYRD

(WOMAN 2)

Lyrics by
RICHARD MALTBY, Jr.

Music by
DAVID SHIRE

WOMAN 2 is seated on a typist's swivel chair at a desk in an apartment building real estate office. Sign on the desk reads "Miss Byrd."
She performs the entire number, including any "dancing," on the swivel chair.

*Throughout, parts in cue-sized notes are merely a suggestion, and performers are encouraged to make the ad lib. scat sections "their own."

He says I'm su - per, too. ___ He calls me hot. I show those base - ment a - part -

___ ments a - lot. ___ Back at work I'm crisp ___ and fresh ___ Re -

li - a - ble Miss Byrd. ___ Seals are danc - ing in ___

___ my flesh, ___ But I don't say a word. I'm show - ing Pent - house "C,"

64

No. 8 THE SOUND OF MUZAK

(COMPANY)

Lyrics by
RICHARD MALTBY, Jr.

Music by
DAVID SHIRE

*Throughout this number, if unable to play these tenths without rolling, transpose bass note up an octave.

84

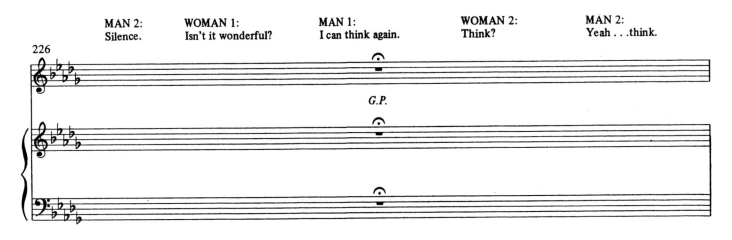

227 Slowly

ALL: *pp*   *sempre accel. e cresc. al fine*

Still you have to ad - mit it's nice

pp sempre accel. e cresc. al fine

232

with mu - sic ev 'ry-

237 *(They plug imaginary wires back into their brains.)*

WOMAN 1. where! Ev - 'ry-

WOMAN 2. where! Mu - sic, mu - sic, mu - sic, Ev - 'ry-

MAN 1. where! Mu - sic, mu - sic, mu - sic, Ev - 'ry-

MAN 2. where! Mu - sic, mu - sic, mu - sic, Ev - 'ry-

(accel. e cresc.)

No.9 ONE OF THE GOOD GUYS

(MAN 1)

Lyrics by
RICHARD MALTBY, Jr.

Music by
DAVID SHIRE

67 Tempo I°

hell, why de-fend all of us good — guys, Stran-gling in plen-ty Yet whin-ing for more?—

71

Truth is, my friend, Just be-tween good — guys, It's not which road you take, Which

Broadening

a tempo—poco rubato

74

life you pick to live in. Which ev-er choice you make, The long-ing is a giv-en. And

poco rall.

77 Meno mosso

that's what brings the ache That on-ly the good guys know.—

ten.

rall. e dim.

No. 10 THERE'S NOTHING LIKE IT

(COMPANY)

Lyrics by
RICHARD MALTBY, Jr.

Music by
DAVID SHIRE

MAN 2 stands at the piano, as if preparing to perform a number in a vocal recital. He gestures that the pianist may begin.

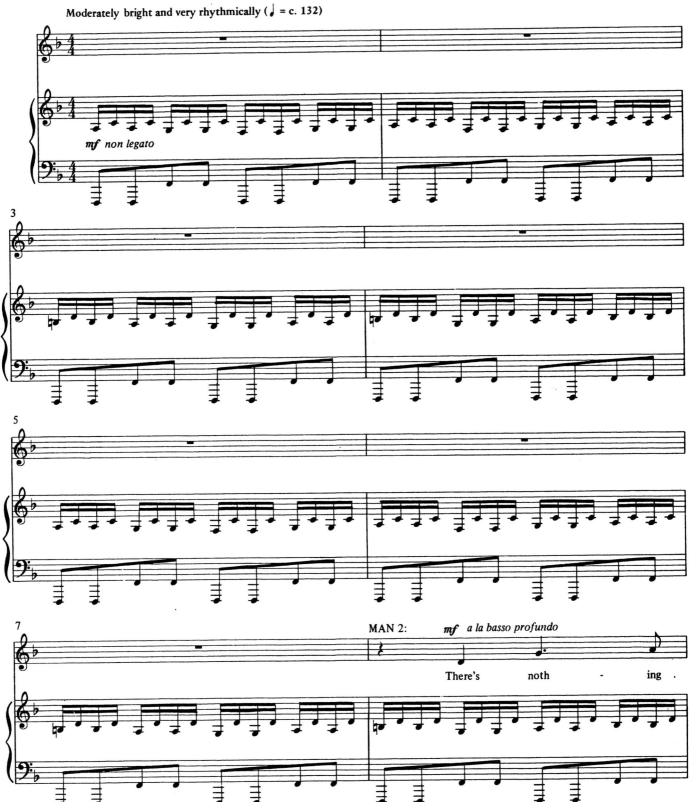

like it. There's noth-ing like it in the

world, _____ This love-ly feel-ing of well-

be - ing. What you're see - ing is a man who's in-cred-i-bly

(Puts a towel around his neck.)

fit. Would you be - lieve it,

That once I weighed two hun - dred fif ty?

I was as pudg - y as a pig. Not just big. I was

fat, I was gross, But now I'm trim and nif - ty. God reached His hand down and

grant - ed me a gif - ty: Health!

(Wearing a towel around her neck)

WOMAN 1:

I feel so

No. 11 LIFE STORY
(WOMAN 1)

Lyrics by
RICHARD MALTBY, Jr.

Music by
DAVID SHIRE

So off he went with his hair of bronze To find a life like Kah-
lil Gi-bran's. I got my rest from the drugs he did. He got his quest, I
got the kid. And oh,
I'm not com - plain - ing.

So I set off— to be a writ - er, —

A mod - ern moth - er on her own.

I wrote up Hap - pen - ings at gal - l'ries,

to surf.___ And oh,___

I was not com - plain - ing.___

So now my son's___ half - way through col - lege.___

I pay tu - i - tion___ like a fine.___

And those sweet young things who hire ___ me now, ___ Those M. B. A.'s mak - ing

fif - ty thou, ___ Who smile and ask what I have done, ___ When they get their jobs from the

fights I won. . . *Aaw, they should all stay home and have babies.*

But I'm not com - plain - ing. ___

Summed up in this no - tion,— I wish I'd stayed with him.

198 Quasi tempo

Lord knows, each day with him was mad - ness,———

sim.

mp

mf (bring out)

202

rall.

As I have spent my life main - tain - ing.——————— But

rall.

206 Very freely

poco ten.

more and more I re - call the joy,— My gold - en dream - er, My lost boy. Our

colla voce

No. 12 NEXT TIME / I WOULDN'T GO BACK

(COMPANY)

Lyrics by
RICHARD MALTBY, Jr.

Music by
DAVID SHIRE

End of Act I

No. 13 THREE FRIENDS
(WOMAN 1, WOMAN 2 and MAN 1)

Lyrics by
RICHARD MALTBY, Jr.

Music by
DAVID SHIRE

This is to be staged as a Vaudeville turn. MAN 1 should play the third (female) friend straight, not in drag or mincing.

Bright "Show-biz" Two (♩ = 156)

Al - ice, the law - yer, An - ge - la, the writ - er,

Nan - cy, the paint - er, Could - n't have been tight - er.

*MAN 1 is playing (and singing) the part of a THIRD WOMAN. Sounds as written throughout.

81 WOMAN 2:
mf
An - ge - la wrote all day in her pa - ja - mas.
mf
85 WOMAN 1:
mf
Nan - cy was paint - ing scen - 'ry at La Ma - mas.
89 MAN 1:
mf
Al - i - ce s crowd took trips to the Ba - ha - mas.
93 ALL:
Off on our own,
Joined at the phone.
f

WOMAN 1
WOMAN 2
MAN 1

Noth - ing in com - mon, But look ___ what we've got. ___

229 cresc.

I would - n't like ___ you if friends ___ we were not, ___ But

233 f

you have me. ___

237 WOMEN 1 & 2:
mf

These are my friends. ___ *You have - n't changed a bit.*

Segue to chaser, as one

No. 13A THREE FRIENDS CHASER
(INSTRUMENTAL)

Music by
DAVID SHIRE

(WOMAN 1, WOMAN 2 and MAN 1 take Vaudeville-style, play-off bows during applause.)

Very fast

No. 14 FANDANGO

(WOMAN 1 and MAN 2)

Lyrics by
RICHARD MALTBY, Jr.

Music by
DAVID SHIRE

(WOMAN 1 goes to BABY)

MAN 2: *mf*

14 WOMAN 1
ba - by. Oh God, I'm sym - pa - thet - ic, My

17
clos - ing's set for two. The buy - er's in from Phoe - nix, My part - ner has the flu. The

20
fact is I was here on the verge of ask - ing you If may - be

23 WOMAN 1:
mf
You'd take the ba - by. Of

26
course, I know what you're do - ing's real - ly vi - tal stuff. I know how much your life's on the

No. 15 THERE
(WOMAN 2 and MAN 3)

Lyrics by
RICHARD MALTBY, Jr.

Music by
DAVID SHIRE

180

No. 16 PATTERNS

(WOMAN 1)

Lyrics by
RICHARD MALTBY, Jr.

Music by
DAVID SHIRE

Freely and reflectively

WOMAN 1:

Pat-terns in my life that I trace ev-'ry day. Pat-terns as I say the things I

al-ways say. Pat-terns in the ceil-ing as I lie a-wake.

Why are pat-terns haunt-ing ev-'ry move I make? Just look: Here I am on

Pat - terns that be - gin as I walk

through a door. Pat - terns in the cur - tains and the

kitch - en floor. Pat - terns in the day's rou - tines I

must ar - range. Pat - terns in the ways I try... but

sempre legato

for Didi

No. 17 ANOTHER WEDDING SONG
(WOMAN 2 and MAN 2)

Music and Lyrics by
DAVID SHIRE

194

No. 18 IF I SING

(MAN 2)

Lyrics by
RICHARD MALTBY, Jr.
and DAVID SHIRE

Music by
DAVID SHIRE

His hands grew numb. And now he can - not play.

I came to vis - it. He sat and asked me, "How could it be this

way?" I could-n't find an an - swer.

I played this tune for him in - stead. My fa - ther sat there smil - ing, For he

for Sally and Bob

No. 19 BACK ON BASE

(WOMAN 2)

Music and Lyrics by
DAVID SHIRE

N.B.: The cue-sized notes in the piano part are to be played on acoustic bass, with WOMAN 2 relating to and interacting with the bass player during the enitre number. The bass player should be onstage with WOMAN 2.

My ba - by plays a line that's — sub - tle, —

Yet — it makes — the strong - est — case. An ar - gu - ment with no re - but - tal —

Got me back on — base. — When — his fin - gers

touch my — strings, — I tin - gle to my — teeth. —

I seem to sing the wild-est things when he is un-der-neath. The on-ly worm that's in this E-den,

Finger snaps

On-ly snag in all this lace, Is where I stand ain't eas-y read-ing

when he's back on bass.

*Ad lib. scat**

(Scat syllables)

(hard Jazz four)

*Throughout, parts in cue-sized notes are merely a suggestion, and performers are encouraged to make the ad lib. scat sections "their own."

No. 20 THE MARCH OF TIME

(COMPANY)

Lyrics by
RICHARD MALTBY, Jr.

Music by
DAVID SHIRE

ALL

59

for the burn - outs. I was - n't read - y for the

64

WOMEN:

MEN:

jokes. I was - n't set for see - ing cel - lu - tite Or

69

ALL:

be - ing par - ent to my folks. I nev - er

74

WOMAN 1,
MAN 1:

WOMAN 2,
MAN 2:

thought I'd go to par - ties _____ And or - der

202 rit. (WOMAN 2 is pushed forward) ♩.=♩ Freely WOMAN 2: mp

Teen - age vi - sion - ar - y,

mf dim. e rit.

mp colla voce

207

Set i - tin - er - ar - y. Got it all like clock - work, Sep - tem - ber bride.

210

Fu - ture mov - ing toward me, Hus - band who a - dored me. Then one aw - ful night he...

213 Più mosso (in 2)

died. And the days seem end - less now. I feel my

222

No. 21 FATHERS OF FATHERS
(MAN 1, MAN 2 and MAN 3)

Lyrics by
RICHARD MALTBY, Jr.

Music by
DAVID SHIRE

earth.

MAN 2: *mf*

Hey, fa - ther, ___ I love you. ___ I pray you'll pull

mf legato

through. You cared for me, It's my turn now To take care of you. I've

cresc.

No. 22 IT'S NEVER THAT EASY /
I'VE BEEN HERE BEFORE

(WOMAN 1 and WOMAN 2)

Lyrics by
RICHARD MALTBY, Jr.

Music by
DAVID SHIRE

When he does, You'll go too. And you'll lose him, _____ now and then.

But each morn-ing _____ start a-gain. And oh, _____ some days you'll be

hap - py. _____ But it won't be eas - y. _____ It's nev-er that eas - y. _____ You think so, but

no, Oh no. I know. _____ It is - n't at

54

And then I ___ see ___ his

57

eyes are gray. ___ Oh ___ God, I've been here be-

61

fore. ___

poco cresc.

65

mf

To want him ___ makes ___ no sense at all. ___

mf

Then ___ we talk and out his feel - ings pour. ___

In - side all ___ my ___ de -

fens - es fall. ___

Oh ___ yes,

I've been here be - fore. ___ The man's all wrong.

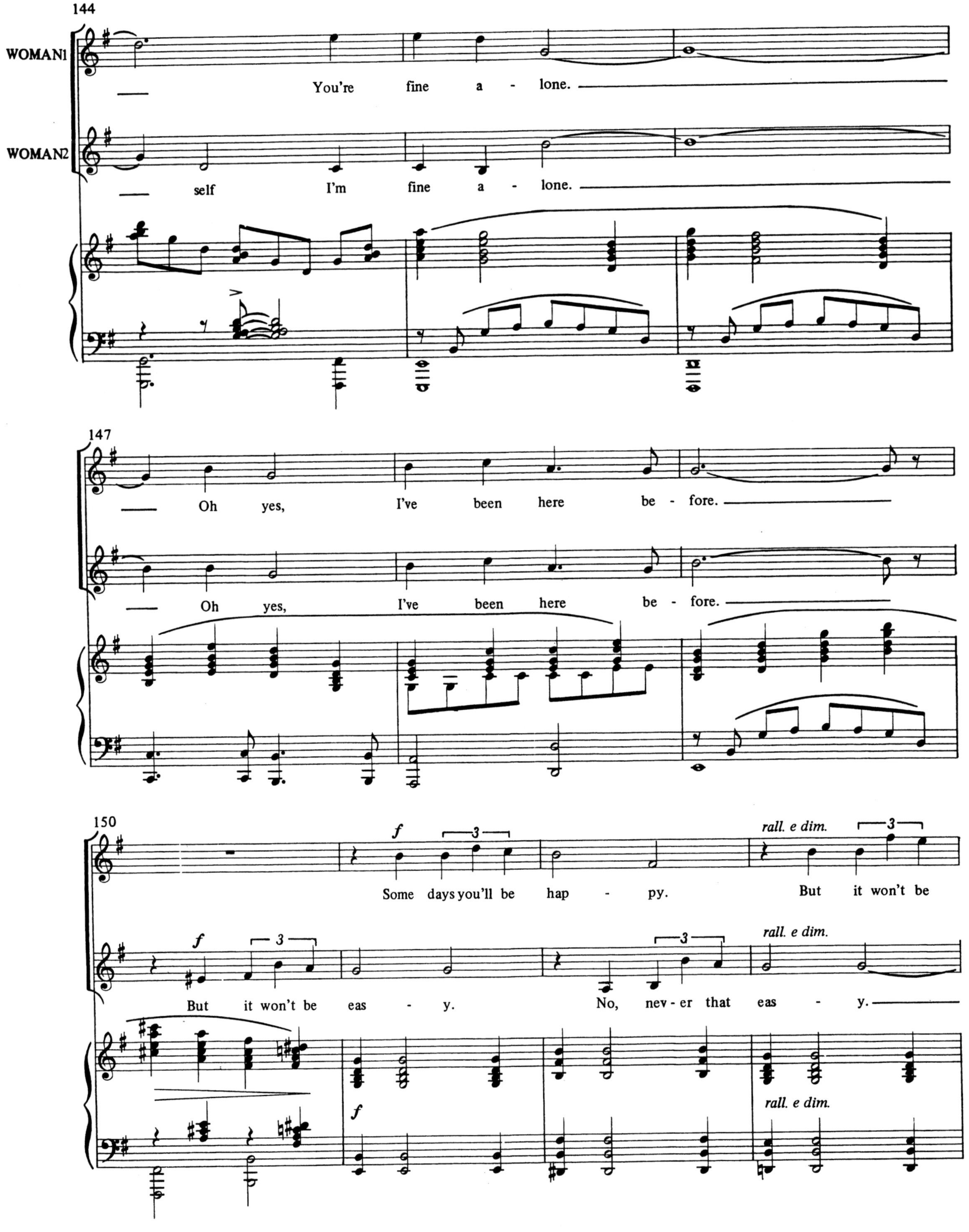
144
WOMAN1
WOMAN2
You're fine a - lone.
self I'm fine a - lone.
147
Oh yes, I've been here be - fore.
Oh yes, I've been here be - fore.
150
f
Some days you'll be hap - py.
rall. e dim.
But it won't be
f
But it won't be eas - y.
No, nev - er that eas - y.
rall. e dim.
f
rall. e dim.

No. 23 CLOSER THAN EVER
(COMPANY)

Lyrics by
RICHARD MALTBY, Jr.

Music by
DAVID SHIRE

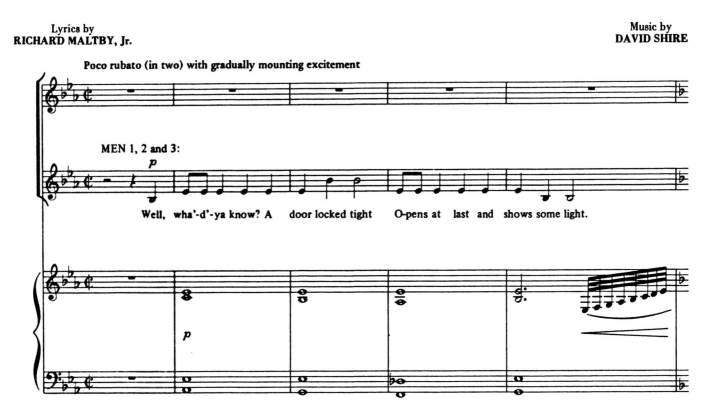

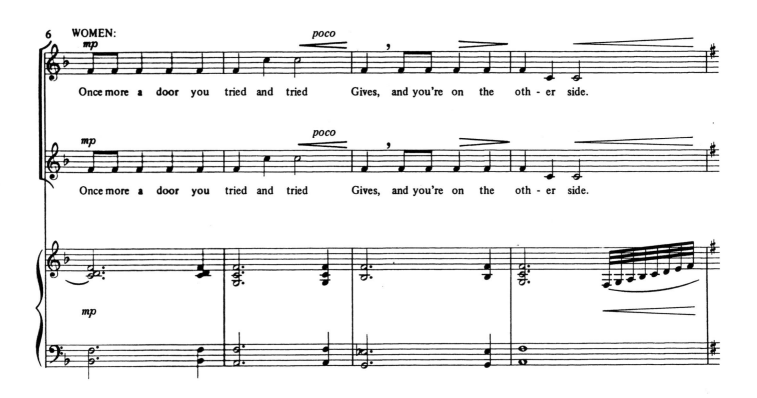

No. 24 FIRST BOWS AND FINALE ULTIMO
(COMPANY)

Lyrics by
RICHARD MALTBY, Jr.

Music by
DAVID SHIRE

No. 25 SECOND BOWS AND EXIT MUSIC

(INSTRUMENTAL)

Music by
DAVID SHIRE

Exit Music
L'istesso tempo

APPENDIX

I'LL GET UP TOMORROW MORNING

(MAN 2)

Lyrics by
RICHARD MALTBY, Jr.

Music by
DAVID SHIRE

Bright (♩ = c. 138)

A COMMUTER is waiting for a train, newspaper under his arm. He looks up the track, looks at his watch, looks at the newspaper. He is a bundle of supressed tension.

(Safety – play at least 3 times)
mf sempre staccato
3
MAN 2: mf
I'm
5
late for work, of course the car won't start.
The
mp
7
brand - new V. C. R. just fell a - part.
I

28
ten year old's best friend is smok - ing pot. The

30
roof will cost a grand I have - n't got. My

32
daugh - ter says the act - ing bug just bit her. My teen - age son is sleep - ing with the

35
sit - ter. I'll get up to - mor - row morn - ing, Make a great big

life. I nev - er know who'll greet me at my

house:— The bro - ker-of - the - month or Min - nie

Mouse. She says she loves her job, and I be -

lieve her. And then she takes a class, and she's this... weav - er.___ I'll

get up to-mor-row morn-ing, Say the past is pre - lude, Stay loose,

Drop a quaa - lude and go on.

At times I think that I am rath - er